Attending the Dying

Attending the Dying
A Handbook of Practical Guidelines

Megory Anderson

morehouse

HARRISBURG • LONDON

Morehouse Publishing, P.O. Box 1321, Harrisburg, PA 17105
Morehouse Publishing, The Tower Building, 11 York Road,
London SE1 7NX
Morehouse Publishing is a Continuum imprint.

Cover design: Thomas Castanzo

Library of Congress Cataloging-in-Publication Data

Anderson, Megory.
  Attending the dying : a handbook of practical guidelines / Megory
Anderson.
    p. cm.
  ISBN 0-8192-2108-2 (pbk.)
  1. Terminally ill—Pastoral counseling of. 2. Church work with the
terminally ill. 3. Death—Religious aspects—Christianity. I. Title.
  BV4338.A54 2005
  259'.4175—dc22

                                              2005004736

Printed in the United States of America

05 06 07 08 09 10   10 9 8 7 6 5 4 3 2 1

TO

the Reverend Lynn Baird and her
extraordinary ministry of pastoral care
at St. Gregory Nyssa Episcopal Church,
San Francisco.

She teaches us, by word and example,
that as our hearts bear witness
to suffering, God is known.

✧ CONTENTS ✦

✦ ACKNOWLEDGMENTS ✦

My profound gratitude goes to Chris Bennett, my friend and colleague, for her many hours of assistance in the creation of this book. Her knowledge and skill are on every page. She will tell you that she is not the expert in the sacred art of dying, but she truly has the higher wisdom. Thank you, Chris.

My thanks also goes to the Reverend Nancy Witt for her contribution of the very practical information in Appendix B, "Recognizing and Understanding the Dying Process." As a health care professional and ordained clergy, she combines very practical medical information with a greater understanding of the spiritual process of dying.

Special thanks to the staff, board, volunteers, and friends of the Sacred Dying Foundation. This work would not be brought to life without their support and hard work.

PART I

The Chaplain/Pastoral Caregiver's Role at the End of Life

✧ CHAPTER 1 ✧

Death as a Sacred Event

I was sitting with an elderly woman who was close to dying. She had been moved from the hospital the week before to a skilled nursing facility. She wasn't strong enough to go home, and they didn't really know what else to do with her. Her name was Ida.

We chatted a bit on and off, but mostly she wanted to sleep. She seemed to find comfort in my holding her very frail hand. It was covered with deep bruises and I held it gently.

Mid-afternoon, a young-looking clergyman came through the door.

"Are you Ida?" he asked. "I'm Jim Robinson, the new assistant at St. Andrew's Church. I heard you weren't feeling well."

Ida opened one eye but then closed it and went back to sleep. I smiled at the man as he pulled up a chair.

Jim began to talk. "Is she asleep? I'm new at the church so I don't know everyone yet. Perhaps I should go. At my last church I was youth director, but at St. Andrew's they have me visiting hospitals and nursing homes."

He looked around nervously. "I think I like kids better than I like hospitals. You aren't expecting them to come in the room, are you, to do shots or needles or anything like that? I'll wait outside if that happens."

I murmured something sympathetically.

He continued. "I had Clinical Pastoral Education in seminary, but mostly I worked with vets and rehab. It was different than this. Hospitals make me nervous."

Ida opened one eye and commented wryly, "It took you long enough to get here."

"Well," he replied, "we're kind of busy at the church. There's Advent coming up and everything."

Ida closed her eyes again, and began talking. "I've been at that church for over sixty years. Don't talk to me about Advent. Why weren't you here before?"

The young priest looked down at the floor. "Ma'am, I got here as soon as I could."

"I was married at that altar," Ida told him, "and I raised my children there. I taught Sunday school, baked pies for the ECW,* and was head of the altar guild for over twenty years. Every time the church needed something, I was there helping out. It was my duty."

She looked at him head-on, her eyes flaming with anger.

"Now that I'm alone and ready to die, you take your sweet time. Just because I can't do all those things anymore, do you think I'm not a member of the church? Sixty years I gave to God at that church, and now you can't bother with me!

"Let me tell you something, young man. You'd better have a better excuse than Advent coming up!"

I chuckled under my breath. This woman was not ready to die yet! As she turned to me and explained, her voice grew a bit calmer.

"In my day," she told me, "the church was everything. We didn't have much religion around the house. Church took care of all that.

---

*Episcopal Church Women

"My children are all grown and moved away. My husband died years ago. I'm all alone. Do you know what that's like? And now this. I know I won't go home. I know I'll die in this bed. What am I supposed to do?"

Her eyes began to fill with tears.

The young clergyman spoke up. "Ma'am, I don't know what you want me to do. I guess I can find a prayer from the Prayer Book. And I can come back on Sunday with communion. Would you like that?"

"Harummph."

"Ida," I said. "Tell us what would make you feel better."

"Communion would help," she said. "But . . . it's not enough. I mean, you young people are always in such a hurry. In and out. The body of Christ and good-bye. I'm dying. Isn't that reason enough to stay a few minutes?"

She looked at me again.

"Your sitting here feels nice. Sometimes I get afraid, and I can feel your hand, and that helps. And when I wake up, maybe I want to hear you tell me things. Like God is waiting for me and it will be all right. Or that I'll see Henry when I finally die. That would give me comfort."

"I have this daughter," she continued. "She lives in Connecticut now. She calls and says hello, and she was here when I first got sick. But now . . . maybe I'd like to tell her some things before I go. I don't think the nurses will help much. But maybe you might," she said to me.

I spoke up. "Of course we'll call your daughter. That's no problem. What else can we do? Maybe someone from the church can come and sit with you. Read to you."

Her eyes brimmed with tears. "I'm so old now, and I'm tired. But I'm afraid to die. What happens? What if I don't go to heaven? What then? Old Reverend Jackson, he would have been here in a flash. But he's long gone. I guess I don't matter anymore." She turned her head into the pillow and I could hear the muffled cries.

I began brushing back her fine grey hair. It was so downy, like a baby's.

"It's all right," I said quietly. "It's all right."

Poor Jim looked so uncomfortable. I noticed, though, that he was carrying a Prayer Book with him.

"Why don't you read something, Jim? Find the Psalms and read to us. It may help."

He leafed through the pages and found what he was looking for. He began reading quietly from those familiar words, "The Lord is my Shepherd. I shall not want. . . ."

As her crying began to soften, I asked Ida, "Can we figure this out together, Ida? Tell us what you need most. Do you want someone with you?"

She nodded. "I feel so afraid," she whispered. "As if no one even cares anymore."

"Jim will talk to people at church," I told her, "and they'll come sit with you."

Jim suggested, "Why don't I call the altar guild? I know they'll be happy to come. You're one of their own. And I'll be by on Sunday after services to bring you communion."

"Ida," I said, "perhaps we can find something for you to hold on to, to remind you that God is with you all the time. He isn't abandoning you, especially now. This is a very special time for you. You are getting ready to meet him."

I looked around the small room. On her bed stand there was a wadded-up linen handkerchief. It had beautiful embroidery around the edges. I opened it up and found a small beaded bracelet. The stones were a lovely shade of deep purple.

"That was my mama's," Ida said.

"It feels so lovely in my hands," I told her as I fingered the beads. "Very soothing. Do you want to hold it?"

She nodded and reached out for it.

"Ida, think about your mother and how much she loved you. She wanted to be with you, so she gave you this bracelet. When you hold it, think about her. Think about how much you're loved."

Ida brought the bracelet to her face and held it against her cheek. As she was cradling it, Jim came over and boldly began to anoint her.

"Ida, this oil is another way to remember how much God loves you. I'm putting it on your head and on your hands. Be protected and guarded as you lie here. Be healed of any pain you have. And remember that you are always in his arms."

There were tears coming down his face as he gently made the sign of the cross on her forehead and hands.

We stayed with her a bit longer as she slept. Her face was peaceful, and I knew it was going to be all right.

"At my last church I was youth director, but at St. Andrew's they have me visiting hospitals and nursing homes." I hear this kind of comment a lot from young clergy. A fundamental shift is occurring in our churches today. In earlier decades, much of the population in our mainline churches were members with young families. Now, many tend to be from an older generation. Our congregations are aging and they are dying. One problem, among many, is that clergy are not prepared to minister to the dying. Seminaries don't teach much beyond how to conduct funerals. There may be a few moments dedicated to pastoral care with the ill and the bereaved, but there is little in our curriculum about care for the dying.

This handbook is designed for any member of the clergy or lay pastoral care worker who is called to be at the side of someone who is dying. There are many other resources available for those who have just received a terminal diagnosis, or for someone who is recently bereaved. This is a handbook for care of the "actively dying," which, in medical terminology, means someone on his or her deathbed.

This work comes out of my own experience with the dying, which I've described in a book called *Sacred Dying: Creating Rituals for Embracing the End of Life*. The book has helped set the stage for an entire paradigm shift in how we, as people of faith, create community and ritual for our dying. I have sat at the deathbeds of more than two hundred people, and learned that there is a tremendous need for sacred presence when someone is at life's end. The church has fallen behind in its ministry to the dying. The Sacred Dying philosophy is that no one should have to die alone and abandoned, and that death is a sacred transition, one filled with grace and mystery. As a community of faith, I believe it is our responsibility to hold the space in which our brothers and sisters make the journey. If we fulfill our responsibility on this end, we can be assured that God will be waiting on the other one.

Throughout history, the community of faith has traditionally been present both physically and spiritually during a death to guide the dying into the afterlife. Only recently, in the age of medicine and technology, have we passed on this responsibility to hospitals and nursing homes. It is time to reclaim death and dying as a spiritual transition.

This handbook is recommended for the chaplain or pastoral care worker as a guide to the process of sitting with someone who is dying, of being spiritually present—of maintaining a vigil—until death occurs. This nuts-and-bolts informational guide for trained caregivers, both lay and ordained, will take you through the stages of the last days and hours of a person's life, answering many common questions and addressing spiritual needs. It suggests ways in which you might also be present after death, commending the soul in its journey to the afterlife and honoring the body left behind. This guide also helps with some difficult issues that can arise, such as how to confront the reality that death is imminent and how to respond to questions about the afterlife.

The guide is organized into three separate sections:

- Part I, "The Chaplain/Pastoral Caregiver's Role at the End of Life," describes what you can do in preparation for a sacred death.
- Part II, "Interacting with the Dying," describes the last stages of death and how you might respond. This includes how to "sit vigil" with the dying person. It also offers suggestions for rituals that might be possible immediately after the death occurs.

- Part III, "Assimilating Your Experience," addresses your own personal needs for reflection and processing after the death occurs.

The appendices offer more tools and information that you might find helpful. Appendix A examines situations that can challenge the chaplain, such as an emergency room death or a death that happens after life-support systems are removed. Appendix B, written by the Reverend Nancy Witt, who, besides being a member of the clergy, is a practicing social worker and a physical therapist, explores in more detail the physical and emotional phases people may experience as they die.

→ CHAPTER 2 ←

Bringing the Sacred to Dying

Those who work with the dying, whether as dedicated career chaplains within a hospital or hospice, or as clergy or laypersons from a congregation within the general community, have a special calling. Being with the dying and their loved ones requires spiritual presence unlike any other.

This guide is based upon several key assumptions. First and foremost, the experience is about a spiritual process that is taking place for the person dying. Dying is often difficult, but it is always sacred. The role of the pastoral caregiver is to help make the dying experience as sacred as possible. No one deserves to die alone and abandoned. One of the key differences that distinguishes the work and philosophy of Sacred Dying from the work done by a hospice or a medical facility is its focus.

Sacred Dying has arisen, in part, out of the necessity to address the particular needs of the person who is actually dying.

The medical community is doing its part to keep patients comfortable and pain free. Medicine focuses on life, on saving life and on prolonging life. When medicine no longer works, hospice may step in. Hospice focuses on the path that leads to death, and eases the person into that transition. As hospice has developed within the Medicare and insurance reimbursement environment in America, the time that hospice workers may spend with the dying person is often limited to proscribed visits, rather than to maintaining a vigil. Some hospice programs have strong volunteer programs that help to fill in the gaps in time with volunteers trained to follow a person through the dying process, and to provide support as they can. But without those volunteers, there is a gap in the continuum of care. And it is into that gap that we go.

It's our job to concentrate on the spiritual process of helping people move from life through death and into the afterlife. We often forget that death isn't just the medical process of the body shutting down—the spiritual process that is occurring at the same time is just as important and powerful. Once we realize that this spiritual process has its own signs and indicators, it is much easier to respond to the dying person's needs for forgiveness and letting go, for assurance of God's love and acceptance, by assuaging fears and anxieties about what is happening and where he or she is going. It is my experience that focusing on love and acceptance, even in the face of anxiety or dread, helps the dying person find the spark of love that is God. Whatever the needs of the dying person, whatever the situation we find ourselves in, this experience belongs to the one dying, and all focus should be on him or her. Being present in this way is often challenging, and it can be tempting to offer a quick fix or a platitude in lieu of real presence. But a quick prayer and laying on of hands doesn't always meet the ultimate needs of the dying.

This leads to our second assumption—that spiritual care at the end of life involves many things, but primarily it means presence. Vigiling[1] with the dying person, providing spiritual presence until the very end, is not only recommended

1. The practice of vigiling with the dying, throughout the dying process and afterwards, is an ancient Christian practice. For an extended description of vigiling and how to put it into practice effectively, see Megory Anderson, *Sacred Dying: Creating Rituals for Embracing the End of Life* (New York: Marlowe & Co., 2003).

but is highly encouraged. If you're a chaplain or serve a busy congregation, you may not be able to sit vigil with the dying for hours at a time. Fortunately, you do not have to do this alone. You can also empower loved ones or family members, in addition to teams of pastoral care-givers, in the practice of Sacred Dying. You then serve as the facilitator guiding others in vigiling. Vigilers can sit quietly with the dying, read Scripture, play music, and use prayer to create sacred presence. It is a powerful ministry and one that can be shared within the community at large.

Preparing to Vigil

As you prepare to sit vigil, it's important to first bring yourself to a sacred place. Since there's no way of knowing ahead of time what the dying person may ask for or need, it is not a time to "plan" your vigil. Rather, you want to become centered and receptive to being 100 percent focused on the dying person's needs. Preparation at this time is about letting go of your own to-do list or agenda and being present to the person who is dying.

- Practice deep and even breathing to calm and focus yourself. Remember, the word inspiration literally means breathing in!
- Purify yourself. Wash your hands and face, not just to disinfect them, but also to wash away other concerns you may be carrying.
- Visualize setting your thoughts and concerns aside to focus completely on the dying person. Leave other things outside.
- Use prayer and meditation to bring yourself to a sacred place so that you can begin the vigil from a centered place.
- Recall any pre-vigil connection or conversations you've had with a dying person: reconnect to the dying person's wishes and needs.
- Pull together/bring appropriate tools (see page 22).

Creating Sacred Space

As a chaplain, you have the ability and the calling to set the stage for a good and holy death. Creating "sacred space" is one of the first steps in setting the environment apart from day-to-day issues, which in turn helps everyone present remember the sacredness of the event unfolding.

Family members and loved ones often take their cues from you, the chaplain. If you honor the space and environment as something set apart, they will realize that the event taking place is holy.

The act of creating sacred space allows for privacy and intimacy; it also defines the physical space so that it can contain the vigil process. Whether you find yourself in a hospital room, a nursing home, or a private residence, the need stays the same: to create and hold a space that is holy in order for this death to happen peacefully. As you create sacred space in the dying person's location, you want to be creative but not intrusive. This is one of the "busy" times of vigiling, when you may be moving or cleaning things. However, this is not about what *you* like or find attractive. From this point on, your role as the chaplain or vigiler is to do what you sense is right for this particular dying person.

- Clear the clutter from the room/space. Straightening the surroundings and opening windows can help make the people involved feel better about the circumstances; the act of cleaning up can give a sense of purpose and helpfulness.

NOTE: be aware of what is clutter and what is there by design.

- Bring in sacred objects. Devotional objects like icons, a rosary, crosses, prayer beads, or significant medallions are important for some people. For others, special objects from their lives, like photographs or even childhood toys, are sacred. Prayer books or books of Scripture are often helpful to have in the sacred space.

- Contain or mark the space. If the dying takes place in a hospital or nursing home room, consider using blankets or curtains. Sometimes candles or lamps in the corners of the room can be used to mark the space, as can incense.

- Sanctify the space. Help everyone present to recognize that this space (and time) is sacred and needs to be treated with reverence. Your instructions don't have to be elaborate; if those gathered are religious, you can ask for God's presence. If not, begin with a simple statement, such as "We are gathered here to help our loved one as she dies."

- Let others know that a vigil is in process, particularly if you're in an institutional setting.

A sign on the door is always appropriate. One nursing home uses a small table with a candle on it outside the door to allow other residents a moment of quiet reflection as they walk by.

Suggested Tools (as appropriate)

- Sheets, blankets, other drapes to create privacy
- Devotional objects
- Objects with personal significance for the dying person
- Furniture, if useful, to mark the space
- Candles or other lights; incense

Building Your Tool Kit

One important responsibility of a chaplain or vigiler is to create your own tool kit to take with you to each vigiling experience. Be prepared to use many of the items or none, depending on the situation. Some of the items in your tool kit may include:

- Candles and matches (useful to set a meditative mood and to create a sacred space)

- Oil, including consecrated oil for anointing and lightly scented massage oil
- Washcloths
- Prayer books
- Prayer cards, readings (collect those that are meaningful to you; they can be laminated)
- Tissues
- Paper to write on and pens/colored pencils
- Special objects, including religious objects or pictures appropriate for a variety of traditions, a large bowl or container, and incense
- A journal you will use to reflect on your vigil experiences
- Music/CDs

The Power of Music

People respond to music on a deep, visceral level, so it is a powerful tool for transition. As with any vigiling tool, come prepared with a musical selection but make the effort to discover what helps the dying person and whether something else might be appropriate.

Personal Memories and Music

Choosing music for a vigil is not about the classics or even about good taste; it is about what is in our consciousness and in our memories, what touches the heart. Some examples include:

- Lullabies or children's songs
- Christmas carols
- Ethnic or patriotic songs
- Religious hymns
- Family favorites

Music and Faith

Almost every faith tradition has prayers set to music or other hymns and songs. There are no instructions for their use, but anyone can:

- Create a family gathering time where music is the main component,
- Use sacred music to bring people together in reverence, and/or
- Bring in musicians and/or singers from congregations.

Secular Music to Evoke Peace

- Meditative or reflective music often leads the listener to a meditative state. It is generally instrumental and relaxing and is often appropriate for a vigil.

- Classical pieces can also have prayer-like qualities; there is no specific list of these, so choose your favorites or discover some of the dying person's preferences ahead of time. In general, look for quieter and more peaceful compositions.

The Power of Ritual

As people representing the faith community, we must recognize the value and power of ritual for the dying process. There are religious rituals from their own traditions that people may desire, such as confession, communion, anointing, and specific prayers and readings from Scripture. Rituals communicate powerfully at times of transition. More personalized rituals can also be used. For instance, if a family member is not able to be present at the bedside, find a photograph or small object that can be included in the family circle to represent the presence of the loved one. Details on how to use ritual creatively are laid out in my book *Sacred Dying*; consult it for specific situations and as a general reference and guide.

Conclusion

Making the shift from being "available" for the family of a person who is dying to being "present" both physically and spiritually with the dying often seems overwhelming. Dying happens under many circumstances and in many ways as the body shuts down. How can we be prepared for them all?

Primarily, we can look within ourselves and try to understand the greater process that is taking place. We are the ones "holding" the space in which a sacred event occurs. We are the watchers in the night. We are the witnesses to an extraordinary act of God. A focused mind-set can help us prepare, and simple tools and presence can help facilitate a good and peaceful death.

PART II

Interacting with the Dying

✧ CHAPTER 3 ✧

Helping Others Prepare

Mrs. Henry has been in the hospital for weeks, and it looks as if she will not make it home. She is in her late eighties, and she knows intuitively that the end is near. Her doctors skirt around the issue, however, and her daughter insists that she will be home in no time.

Mr. White refuses to admit that he is terminally ill. The doctor and his family all have tried getting him to talk about what is happening to him, yet he turns away and refuses to communicate.

When the elderly Mrs. Lee is hospitalized, her eldest son becomes the communicator and decision-maker for the whole family. "In our culture," he explains, "it is bad luck to tell the elder that she is dying. We cannot speak of it."

For the most part, our society tries to avoid death, even when it is clearly near. I have come upon many situations where the patient knows intuitively that he or she is dying. In fact, after perhaps months of treatment and dearly held hopes for recovery, there is often a moment of sudden realization, "Oh my God, I'm dying!" Take advantage of that realization to begin the conversation. There is a lot of work to do, emotionally as well as spiritually, when death is imminent, and that work is often frightening, especially if the person has not been accustomed to confronting spiritual issues. The Buddhists teach us that we should live our entire lives in preparation for the moment of death; unfortunately, we have not taken their wisdom to heart. Many start their spiritual journeys in the eleventh hour.

What Do I Do When the Conversation Arises?

Get whatever practical information you can from medical personnel and/or the family now that death is coming. Find out as much about the family and the cultural context as possible; this will be different every time because it's completely subjective, so ask!

There are really two conversations you may need to have:

1. *With family/friends.* You may have to deal with denial or irrational belief in recovery. Sometimes the family is unwilling to address death as a reality (for example, in Asian cultures it's inappropriate to discuss death directly). Helping the family realize that the patient already knows he or she is dying may be the key to open communication. There may be things the patient wants to express to the family. Unfinished business is always important in the dying process, and you may be able to help facilitate it.

Keep in mind that this process is about the dying person. If a family member or loved one wishes to "unburden" him- or herself, ask if it will serve the purpose of helping put things to rest, or if it will only cause pain and harm. Whose need does it serve? If it does not help the dying person, try to steer the loved one to other means of confession.

2. *With the dying person.* Ironically, this conversation may often be more realistic than the discussions with family members. The patient is

sometimes ready and even eager to have an
honest conversation about his or her impending
death. "What will happen to me?" "What does
dying feel like? Will it hurt?" "Tell me what God is
going to do when I die." Sometimes this conversation is very practical, and you need to allow the
person to think through whatever issues he or she
needs to address. At other times, the conversation
becomes very spiritual and focuses on what will
happen in the afterlife. Another possible reaction
the dying person may have is a feeling of paraly-
sis. It is important to find out why. What is the
block? Is it anger? Does the patient not want to
leave loved ones behind? Does the feeling have to
do with fear of God and judgment?

Once you've determined it's time for a conversation, here are some helpful ways to begin:

- What do you think is going to happen to you?
- What do you think/believe about the
  afterlife?
- When you think about dying, what
  concerns you the most?

Your job is to uncover issues, blockages, and unfinished business. You don't know what you'll

hear, but some common themes include: fear, anger, remorse, family relationships, guilt/judgment, and God.

Most people leave their unresolved issues until the last days and then panic. One of the goals of the Sacred Dying process is to help people begin to deal with their spiritual issues before impending death.

Religious and Family Dynamics

Religious and Cultural Context

Understanding the dying person's religious and cultural traditions is critical to creating a Sacred Dying experience. We cannot make assumptions about a person's background and beliefs, even if he or she is a long-time member of a congregation or is affiliated with a particular denomination. Faith and how a person expresses beliefs and practice are often subject to life experiences. Faith is seldom guaranteed and definitive. On the deathbed, especially, a person is often faced with many unique fears and doubts.

It is vital to ask questions, even if someone's religious or cultural beliefs seem obvious. Find out:

- How have culture and religion shaped the person's life?
- What are the family variations within the religious tradition?
- Are religious beliefs consistent within the family?
- Are there specific traditions in the family/culture for honoring the body after death?
- If there has not been a lifelong connection to religion, does the person wish to reconnect or not?
- What are the significant religious and cultural symbols for the family?

In every action and question, your goal is to express: "I want to honor your beliefs and practices to make dying sacred for you." Mirror the dying person's language and tone to emphasize acceptance. Respect the person's beliefs and desires to use the language/symbols/rituals of the tradition. Be careful about pushing your own doctrine and beliefs on a person who has chosen a different path.

The Afterlife

Many times, a dying person's specific religious interest focuses on the afterlife. In general, you are likely to find one of two "categories" of religious belief about the afterlife:

1. Belief in heaven, hell, and perhaps purgatory, or in a moment of judgment (Judaism, Christianity, Islam); or

2. Belief in reincarnation or in a cycle of life, death, and rebirth (Hinduism, Buddhism, neo-paganism).

There is also a third category called "I don't know what to believe."

Support whatever afterlife beliefs the dying person holds, even if they are ambiguous. Talk about words and symbols that come up, using the person's own language and symbols in your conversation. Be sensitive to specific issues, for example:

- whether the person believes he or she will see family members after death or not,
- finding a place away from pain and tiredness, and
- finding a place of joy, happiness, and rest.

There may be a feeling of panic or fear about pain, punishment, or judgment in the afterlife. Be as reassuring as possible, helping the person find love as he or she dies.

A deathbed vigil is *not* the time to engage in theological or doctrinal challenges. People who are about to face death and the afterlife do not generally want a theological discourse. They want reassurances of God's mercy, love, and acceptance.

Challenges

Q: What if someone else in the room insists on imposing conflicting religious beliefs?

A: Remember that this time is about the person dying. While it is important to respect all beliefs, it is often appropriate to ask someone to pray in another room.

Q: What if the dying person does not have any religious beliefs?

A: Being present at the end of life is about creating a space for sacred dying, which is not necessarily religious. Whether or not the dying person has established religious beliefs, we can always create a sacred place for him or her.

Q: What do we do about fear of judgment, or going to hell?

A: It is always appropriate to speak of God's love and mercy. Confession, especially in the Abrahamic faiths, is part of the last rites and can be used to relieve anxiety about things weighing on the dying person's conscience. When using rituals of reconciliation, try to put specific issues to rest and then move the conversation to God's mercy and forgiveness.

Family Dynamics

At times, you may vigil with someone who is dying alone; if so, the choices you make will be determined by you and the dying person.

However, you are likely to sit vigil in situations where loved ones and friends are occasionally or always present. In this case, the role of the chaplain or the vigiler is more complex and can become challenging. From a long-lost sibling to a detached spouse, from an "enthusiastically religious" relative to a deeply concerned and involved spouse, the expectations of family members are wide-ranging. While family and friends will be experiencing their own grief and letting-go process, your role is to remain supportive yet neutral.

Fundamentally, however, the chaplain and ultimately the vigiler are present to create a sacred experience for the dying person. Unlike other professionals and volunteers, your primary focus is on the needs of the person moving from life to death. To the extent that the family can be positively involved in that transition, invite them in.

In Judaism and Buddhism, for instance, the teachings say that the dying process is so spiritually important that whenever family members become too distraught, they should be asked to leave the deathbed room until they can pull themselves together. If, in the process of vigiling, sacred space has been created and the room is filled with a prayer-like atmosphere, you will want to keep the family grounded in that prayer-like space.

Sometimes a family member may need to be distracted and led to another room. Consider encouraging him or her to take a break, such as getting a cup of tea or going for a walk. If you are working with others, this is a good way to divide the work. Remember that as a chaplain or a vigiler, you are an invited guest, but also keep in mind that a gentle nudge can make a big difference.

Challenges

Q: What if family members begin to argue or raise their voices?

A: Ask them firmly to take their discussion outside the room.

Q: What if I'm asked to leave by a family member?

A: Suggest that you will stay with the dying person while the family discusses this as a group outside the sacred space. Then respect their ultimate wishes.

✧ CHAPTER 4 ✧

The Dying Process

"We really can't do anything more," the physicians say. "Perhaps you might want to consider hospice, or the palliative care unit." Or: "We can make you comfortable; there are all sorts of pain medications for a time like this."

So you, the patient, and his or her loved ones know that death will occur and that there is little the medical community can do. No one can tell you when or how soon the death will happen or what it will look like. The family often feels a sense of frustration and helplessness. Time, in a sense, is behaving normally. The days go by and people wait, not knowing when and how things may take place. The dying person often drifts in and out of consciousness, sometimes wonderfully lucid, at other times deep in sleep. Perhaps there is pain and restlessness, or perhaps there is just a feeling of waiting. Every death process is different, and chaplains come into the picture at different stages each time.

Stage 1: Lucid but Approaching Death

If you are able to meet the dying person and his or her loved ones at this point in the dying process, a lot can be accomplished. It is a time when you can facilitate the dying process with meaningful in-depth discussions, reconciliations, and rituals. Usually, the dying person has begun to look death in the face and has many concerns about it. Families are also trying to accept the fact that death will happen shortly. Everyone is—or should be—concerned about what is best for the dying person. It is a time to put things in order: papers and documents, conversations with loved ones, and anything else left "undone." It is also a time to examine relationships with loved ones and with God.

What to Expect

- What is happening to the body physically can vary widely depending on the cause of impending death: it's especially important to touch base regularly with the medical staff.
- What is happening to the dying person emotionally can vary depending on the level of inner acceptance and external support. Feelings such as anger, fear, guilt, relief, and discomfort with unfinished business are common.
- Spiritually, the dying person is entering the transition phase, asking questions, and wanting to get his or her life and relationships in order.

Timing is very fluid for this phase: it can go on longer or take less time than expected. The best approach is to help get personal things in order. Be present but don't be surprised if this phase takes a while. Have someone keep in touch daily to watch for signs of active dying (see page 49). Waiting, and not knowing, is often the hardest part about this phase.

Conversations with the Dying Person

Your interaction with the dying person should be accepting, curious, and respectful. Use your intuition and inner wisdom during the vigiling process to make it a sacred death experience. There really is no checklist for being with the dying; the situation relies both on your past experiences as well as on your ability to be fully in the moment on behalf of the dying person. However, there are some things to consider:

- Be aware of your assumptions! For example: "Everyone needs to confess before dying."
- Pay attention to people's words as they speak about the transition: Are they headed for the "pearly gates"? Do they want to "go home"? Oftentimes, a dying person will recount dreams or visions of loved ones who have already died. Be present and supportive. You are helping him or her prepare for the death transition.

During this stage, people often ask, "What's going to happen next?" When people are dying and the afterlife is just days or even hours away, they don't want to hear theology. They want their questions answered and their fears assuaged. They often want to know that someone will be with them and that they will not be abandoned. Some common things people say include:

- "I've tried to do good things and be a good person. But now what?"
- "I believe in Jesus and I know I am saved."
- "Do you think my husband will be waiting for me in heaven?"
- "I'm Jewish, and we don't talk about heaven or hell. Do we?"
- "I was taught that if I ever stopped going to church, I would go to hell."
- "I've done things I'm ashamed to think about. What's going to happen to me?"
- "I believe in reincarnation. I know my soul will go on to another life."
- "I've loved God my whole life, and now I will finally be with him."

Reinforce the positive. When negative things come up, you can say "none of us knows" and help the dying person find a place of love. When questioned about your own personal beliefs, be honest and say what you believe—but be positive and supportive.

Help evoke memories, including family and friends, in the process as appropriate. Be sure there's an opportunity for family and friends to say good-bye. You may be involved in creating a structure for that event, or you may need to allow private space and excuse yourself.

Continue to communicate even if the dying person is unconscious. Sacred presence is always important. Be careful what you say around the bedside, even if the person is asleep or unconscious; always assume that the dying person takes everything in.

NOTE: If the dying person comes from your belief tradition, now is a good time to reinforce teachings/beliefs and pull from your specific Scripture and prayers . . . but be careful about assuming he or she agrees. Ask first.

Conversations with Family and Friends

Help everyone involved to pull together and focus on the dying person and his or her needs. Try to help the loved ones see that this time isn't about their needs as much as it is about the dying person's needs. You may need to ask family members to "take it outside." The football game on television usually does not create a sacred environment.

Do family counseling as needed to facilitate resolution, but be careful about whose agenda you are being asked to address. If the proposed intervention/discussion is not going to aid in a good death for the patient, ask the family member to discuss things with you later. The bottom line of this phase is to help the dying person shift from fighting to live to preparing to die.

Putting Affairs in Order

When people are dying, their natural response is to want to put their affairs in order. Some people focus on the practical details of life—wills, bequests, family affairs. Others focus on putting personal relationships in order or on tending to their relationship with the Divine.

Process/Actions

Rituals can help the dying person move through reconciling life and relationships. Some rituals that are appropriate at this stage include formal or religious rituals (which will often require clergy), such as:

- Rites of anointing
- Prayers of healing
- Confession/reconciliation
- Purification rituals (e.g., baptism)
- Communion

Individual or personalized rituals can include rituals that deal with:

- *Anger.* Since anger is a physical emotion, rituals releasing anger are often physical. Try to think of ways to help capture those visceral feelings and bring them outside the person. Sometimes this may entail destroying objects; at other times, it may involve hitting or punching symbols of the object of anger.
- *Fear.* Death is movement to an unknown land, which can be frightening. Assuaging fear often involves providing comfort and assurance of safety and love, including finding something that is comforting to the individual.

- *Guilt.* When a person is dying, guilt over wrongdoing can weigh heavily on his or her conscience. When a person wants to make things right, asking and receiving forgiveness is extremely important.

Remember that rituals are part of the process, not necessarily an indicator that death is imminent. Be careful of developing an attitude such as, "You've had the last rites, you have said your good-byes; now it's time to die." Recognize that timing happens for a reason. A person may be holding on for a variety of reasons. Maybe the body isn't ready to shut down yet or maybe the dying person has more issues to address. It may even be that fear is taking over. Use your intuition to discern what is nature's course and what may be fear or dread; you can't do anything about the former, but you can help enormously with assuaging the person's fears and doubts.

Stage 2: Actively Dying

Carol is in her bed in the palliative care unit at the hospital. She is curled up in a fetal position and unconscious. Her breathing for the past twelve hours has been erratic, which scares her husband and children. She gasps for breath, lets it out, and then it seems as if she stops breathing altogether. Then, after what seems like forever, she gasps for air again. The nurses tell the family that this is normal.

She was restless throughout the night, grasping and pulling at the sheet, often mumbling to herself. Her hands and feet are ice cold. "It won't be long now," the nurse says.

When the body begins to shut down and death is imminent, whether it takes a few hours or even a day or two, very specific and recognizable signs appear. At this stage, known as "active dying," nurses or caregivers present will say things like, "He doesn't have long now. Call the family." Spiritually, vigiling should occur at this point.

In the Jewish tradition, which gives us wonderful insight into what the process can be for loved ones as well as for the dying person, the one who is actively dying is called the "gossess."

A shift happens. From the beginning of an illness, the Jewish community prays for healing and a return to a healthy life for the person. Later, we see the prayers move to the language of "may it be God's will that this person should recover, but if it is not God's will . . ."

As the person moves into the gossess stage, everything changes. We recognize that death is about to occur, and we must prepare the gossess as well as the loved ones. People are called in immediately to begin continuous prayers. The room is changed into a place of prayer. Psalms are read by members of the family or by the community. There is a beautiful prayer of confession in Hebrew called the "Vidui," which is recited: "May You heal me completely, but if it is Your will that I die from this illness, then I accept Your decree . . ."

During this period, the focus should be on the needs of the dying person. Jewish texts state that if anyone is overwhelmed with grief during this time, he or she must leave the deathbed room to compose him- or herself. It is critical that no one should upset the dying person and this very sacred act. Both the family and the community are responsible to see that death is sacred.

As a chaplain, regardless of faith or cultural traditions, once it is clear that death is imminent, you should be present to facilitate the transition from one state of being to the next. This moment is sacred and powerful. Use this time to help make the shift to the sacred happen for the family and loved ones by continuing to be present for the dying person and by acknowledging the sanctity of the transition he or she is experiencing.

Help the family focus all of their attention on the person dying as they gather together. Tell them that this is a special time of quiet and calm, a space for prayer and meditation. Use the room as a place of prayer. Turn off the television. Ask that trivial or inappropriate conversations be held outside the room. You can guide the family to sit quietly, listen to soft music, offer prayers, or speak quiet words of love for the dying person.

Understanding the physical process of dying is central to our own comfort level as we work with the dying. As the body's complex systems cease to run, there are "soft signs of dying." While the timing of death is not entirely predictable, as more and more of these signs are present, death is more imminent (usually within a few days).

What to Expect Physically*

1. A loss of vital energy resulting in increasing periods of sleepiness and weakness.
Possible responses:

- Support the need for sleep by helping to create a peaceful atmosphere.
- Continue to communicate with the person, even if he or she is in a coma.
- Help with previously independent tasks, such as making the person comfortable in the bed or assisting with sips of water.

2. Changes in breathing patterns are common, and may include irregular breathing, panting, gasping, and sighing. There may also be congestion, which is sometimes called the "death rattle." Possible responses:

- Reassure the dying person and loved ones that everything is all right.

---

* See Appendix B for an in-depth description of physical signs of pending death.

- Request assistance from the nurse or care-giver if necessary to help make the person comfortable.

3. Changes in the nervous system can include diminished senses, hallucinations, and less feeling in the extremities. Be aware that hearing is generally the last sense that remains. Possible responses:

- Allow enough light to see.
- Speak clearly.
- Make sure the environment is controlled to minimize stimulation.

4. Changes in circulation and temperature regulation can include temperature swings up or down, extremities feeling cool to the touch, and swelling. Possible responses:

- Reassure the dying person and loved ones that everything is all right.
- Apply a cool washcloth to the forehead or add a warm blanket.
- Make the person as comfortable as possible.

5. Changes in appetite might include waning hunger and thirst and difficulty swallowing. Possible responses:

- Don't be overly concerned: a person does not die because he or she stops eating. People stop eating because they are dying.
- Provide small amounts of some favorite foods or liquids.
- Do not force consumption.

6. Changes in bowel and bladder function include constipation or cessation of bowel function, reduced urine output, and, toward the end, incontinence. Possible responses:

- Encourage scrupulous hygiene for comfort.
- Ask the nursing staff or caregiver to provide a commode or catheter if needed.
- Place a pad underneath the dying person.

What to Expect Spiritually and Emotionally

Many actively dying people become far less anchored in the present, and can seem to be experiencing a different time period. For example, they may be back in their childhoods, having conversations with their mothers or childhood friends, or they might be reexperiencing times when they were particularly happy, such as courtship and early marriage. It is not at all unusual for actively dying people to have what seem to be incoherent conversations with people in the room, often directed at the ceiling or toward high corners of the room. Many people see these experiences as having one foot in this world and one foot in the next. Possible responses:

- Support the dying person where and when he or she is.
- Ask questions to encourage sharing.
- Know that the mind and spirit are still active.
- Realize that the experiences are quite real, and can often give those witnessing the death a glimpse into another world.

A dying person's focus frequently turns inward. As the body begins to shut down and the soul begins to separate, the person often needs to address things that will give him or her strength for the journey. Dying people almost always feel a very real concern about the afterlife: "What is happening to me?" Be reassuring. They will often be concerned about last wishes. Possible responses:

- Help the person express things he or she needs to say.
- Recognize that you may be the only person who hears and honors his or her final words.
- Acknowledge and affirm the dying person's final wishes.

While some people want someone with them for comfort, others may have a strong need for privacy. Possible responses:

- Base your actions on what the dying person wants; some people need to be alone to focus on what is happening to them. However, stay close by and check in regularly.
- Know the difference between the need for privacy and letting the person go through this experience alone. Help family members and loved ones recognize that the patient may need privacy, and that it is perfectly fine to leave the room. Many times

family members feel terribly guilty for not being present at the moment of death ("I left the room for only a minute to get something to drink!"), but often a dying person will choose that exact moment to let go and die. It is a question of privacy, and nothing more.

After the Tasks: Vigiling Begins

When the tasks are done and people have said what they needed to say, we often move into a quiet time of waiting. The dying person slips into sleep; the body begins to shut down. It may take a short period of time or it may take hours. Frequently, family members or loved ones may feel uncomfortable. "What do I do? Do I just sit here waiting for her to die?"

And the answer is yes. We sit and wait for death to happen.

There are several ways to be present during the last hours of the vigiling. You can offer to sit quietly in the background while family members are present. If family members feel more comfortable coming and going, you can offer to be the one at the bedside. Take your cues from the loved ones.

If you are the person sitting vigil, use this time to create a quiet presence for everyone. Quiet presence is more than an absence of movement and noise; it truly is an active state. Even when you are still, you can meditate and pray. Continue to hold an image of what the dying person wants and needs. In other words, your spiritual presence can bring peace and receptivity.

Process/Actions during Vigiling Time

- Focus on and listen to the dying person. If he/she wants to talk, be available; if not, be silent.
- Stillness and silence are the cornerstones of sitting vigil. Most of the time spent in a vigil is just waiting and watching, listening and praying.
- Do not have the television blaring or be swayed by other distractions. Use reading, music, and discussion with intention, not as ways to "fill time."
- Use prayer and meditation to keep the space sacred. Invite the dying person to join you in prayer and meditation.

- Be aware that most people die during the night. As a vigiler, you may want to take over while loved ones/friends sleep.
- Use your intuition when something out of the ordinary arises.

Readings

- Readings are often based on religious and cultural beliefs and practices. Consider Scripture and prayers.
- Other options are poetry, writings of special significance to the dying person, or messages from family members to the dying person.
- Children's books are often very special.
- Part of the vigiling time may be spent reading to yourself or journaling about your experience.

Setting

To the extent of your ability, try to create a setting that is conducive to quiet presence. Consider ways to limit noise and interruption, such as dimming the lights or partially closing a door or curtain, and encourage others who come into the sacred space to respect its sanctity.

Tools Used (as appropriate)

- Prayer cards, books with readings (possibly laminated cards of some favorites)
- Incense
- Soft, meditative music
- A journal
- Rituals from your religious tradition appropriate for the last moments

Stage 3: The Moment of Death

Each faith tradition believes that at the time of death, the soul leaves the body. Where the soul goes differs according to the religious belief, but this moment of departure is a sacred event, and one that requires not only respect from the living, but also assistance from those who witness it.

In our secular society, once death occurs, the body is viewed as something to be shunned or to be afraid of. This has not always been the case, especially within religious communities. Most traditions have specific rituals once the soul has left the body. Some of the rituals last a few moments and, once those are over, they become rites for purifying and honoring the body. One moves quickly into the next.

By honoring the moment of death, you promote the continuity between life and death. The flow from life to death is not always an exact, precise moment—it tends to be fluid, just as the soul, in the hours before death occurs, moves in and out of the body.

What to Expect

The moment is happening—death is at hand. Breathing has changed, and then suddenly it has stopped. Everything is different. You can feel it physically in the room; perhaps the light has changed; perhaps it is the temperature of the air. Some people see a light flicker, or the curtains at the window sway back and forth.

Some people will go to the window and crack it open so the soul can depart. Some people will light a candle and put it at the head of the bed of the person who has just died. Some who practice Judaism or Islam may want to move the body to the floor, facing Jerusalem or Mecca.

There are many traditions that mark the moment of death—A blessing: "The Lord giveth and the Lord taketh away; Blessed be the Name of the Lord"—A commendation: "Go forth, Christian soul, from this world . . ."

Take the opportunity to spend time in quiet reflection and prayer. Don't feel you have to act right away, especially by moving the body away from family and loved ones. The vigiling is not yet over.

Conversations with Family and Friends

Let people know that, as death draws closer, they may experience a change in the room temperature or physical sensations. Many feel as if the dead person were looking down or were still in the room.

Continue to keep the space sacred, including your communications with staff from the facility. Have the death legally documented, but maintain the vigil process. Be a liaison for the family—hold off having the body taken away too quickly.

Rituals Appropriate at This Stage

- Ritual prayers of commendation.
- Making changes to the body—closing the eyes, folding the arms, rearranging the bed,

and sometimes moving the body to another position.

- Religious and cultural traditions used for the moment of death. Ask what the family's traditions are and follow them.

Process/Actions

- Take time and don't make an abrupt transition.
- Death is more than just a monitor going off or the last breath. The place of death is still a sacred space.
- Talk with the staff regarding your plans if you are in an institution; expect a hospital or nursing home to allow about an hour before the body needs to be moved.
- Find the caregiver or nurse who has been responsible for the physical needs of the dying person to help with the natural bodily functions that may occur after death. If you are alone, be aware of these processes and have cloths or pads nearby.
- Recognize the "practical person" among the loved ones who will call hospice and relatives.

- If hospice care is involved, make the call to notify them.
- If you are at a home and do not want the body moved right away, postpone calling 911 or the funeral home for a little while.

Many believe that the soul is in a state of extreme flux during this period of detachment, which may last for some time. Spend this time in quiet prayer.

The body is sacred and needs to be honored and purified. Some spiritual traditions have very specific instructions for the care of the body immediately after death. Options include:

- Marking the change by relaxing or covering/clothing the body.
- Using a symbol to mark the change in status of the body: a light (Judaism) or flowers (Hinduism).
- Moving the body to the floor.
- Ritual washing.

The location where death took place has also been altered by virtue of the death. Changes can be made to the room to signify that death has occurred, such as rearranging significant items or opening curtains.

Stage 4: After Death (Time with the Body)

Mark Lee practiced Tibetan Buddhism, and before his death, he explained to his friends that he wanted his body to be kept in his bed throughout the night. "Watch and pray," he told those who took turns caring for him during his illness. He explained to them how he believed the soul needed help to find its way into the afterlife. His friends did as he asked, and they found the quiet hours of the night watch with Mark's body eerily comforting.

In many cultural and religious traditions, sitting with the body after death is an important part of the transition from life to death. Though our culture has not traditionally supported this view, people who experience sitting vigil with the body often feel it is an incredibly moving and important experience. It is a time when loved ones can say good-bye. People often experience the change in body temperature and physicality. Someone once put it, "I actually knew, halfway into the night, that the soul had gone, and that the body was just an empty shell."

Your role as a chaplain in cases where this might be a new and unaccustomed idea is to be a facilitator and supporter. Continue to hold the moment sacred. Encourage family members to stay longer with the body as appropriate.

This is a time of transition as you begin to hand things off to the family and make your exit. You're moving from being part of the process to helping loved ones continue in the way that makes sense for them.

Process/Actions

Talk over various options with the loved ones. These options may include:

- Doing a vigil while the body is at home. The time frame can be an hour, or extend throughout the night until sunrise.
- Calling the funeral home and creating a vigil there.
- Allowing the family to decide the length of time spent with the body. It is not

your choice, but you can offer information and suggestions.

Sacred Time with the Body

This time of staying with the body occurs either
at home or at a funeral home. The most important aspect of this time is calm and quiet to allow
for reflection, remembrance, and communion.
The experience is very special for many people,
and they often reflect that the soul seems close by
while they sit with the body. Many comment that
there's a profound physical change after a couple
of hours, almost as though the "lights go out"
and it's just a body.

Process/Actions

- A space apart allows time for the closest
  family members and loved ones to sit
  with the body privately (never more than
  a few people).
- A prayer vigil for the family allows a time
  for good-byes, an acknowledgment of God,
  or even a personal reaction to the death.

- This after-death vigil can be a time to wash and purify the body, or even to clothe the body as a way for people to pay respect. Many religious traditions and cultures have formal rituals that are prescribed.
- As loved ones say good-bye, grief and sadness are a part of this vigil time. It is still a transition time between a focus on the dead person and on the needs of loved ones.
- The transition from life to death takes time. Most beliefs state that the soul/spirit is still in the room for a period after the body actually dies. Honor that. Pray that the soul becomes united with God, moving to a fuller place.

Closure

Closure is a chance to thank, in a spirit of gratitude, the divine presence, others who have participated, and the person who has died, for the sacred experience you have all shared.

Process/Actions

- It may be most appropriate for you to slip away quietly.
- Other possible expressions of closure include offering thanks, breaking the circle of people around the bed, moving outside the sacred space, or returning the space to its normal state.
- Inviting those who wish to continue to sit in silence. The silence that accompanies death is especially sacred; respect it.
- Leaving contact information or offering referral information, as appropriate.

Conclusion

Being witness to a death is a profound experience for everyone—for family members and loved ones and for health care professionals who have cared for the patient—and certainly for the person who ministers spiritually. When you have sat vigil with a dying soul, you are forever changed. You have experienced a great mystery.

The role of vigiler is one that is historical. The role of the watcher, the spiritual guide, is one of honor. In this modern age, when the medical community directs most of the dying process, the role of spiritual guide for the dying needs to be reclaimed. We need to hold our position not only within the existing structure of the medical communities who treat the terminally ill, but also within our spiritual and religious communities that have forgotten its value. This is the new paradigm. We are in the process of reconnecting with what has been forgotten about Sacred Dying from the past and ensuring that it is valued and used in the future.

PART III

Assimilating Your Experience

✦ CHAPTER 5 ✦

Personal Processing
and Reflection

Every pastoral caregiver knows how difficult it is to become intensely involved in the life of a patient or a member of the congregation, especially when the person is in crisis. There are decisions to be made and intense emotions involved. Professional training teaches you how to become objective in order to be an effective minister or counselor. But being spiritually present with the dying calls for a new paradigm of participation. You must enter into that sacred place with the dying person and walk with him or her through the dying experience. Preparing yourself spiritually is important as you begin that journey, and it is just as important to take care of yourself after the death takes place.

Everyone who participates in a Sacred Dying vigil is affected by the experience, and the vigiler is no exception. Each death vigil will bring its own lessons and challenges. It is vital for your spiritual and emotional health that you allow time and space for your own transition.

The most important thing to realize after sitting vigil is that you are in an altered state, slightly disconnected from the world and the people around you. You should not jump immediately back into your normal routine or expose yourself to lots of sensory input. If possible, keep things around you gentle and calm while you process your experience.

Process/Actions

- Recognize that you may need some in-depth transition time.
- Take a walk, preferably in a peaceful and/or beautiful place.
- Take time personally to journal about these questions:

How did I feel about this vigiling experience?

How am I spiritually with this vigiling experience?

How did this vigiling experience work logistically?

How did I interact with family members and loved ones?

What did I learn from this vigiling experience?

- Take a shower/perform some cleansing rituals.
- Go to bed.
- Be careful about holding conversations immediately after a vigil (although you may need to talk with someone to express your thoughts and feelings about the vigil).
- Be sure you're okay to drive before you get in a car.
- Continue to take things gradually, exposing yourself to the world consciously.
- Learn and respect your own unique transition preferences (being alone or talking, walking or being still, etc.).

Conclusion

The focus for those who participate in the work and ministry of Sacred Dying is to be present for and to support the dying person through the final hours and moments of his or her life in such a way that the process is as sacred as possible. It is in learning about this process, then, that we gain confidence and can be present to comfort and support the person who is dying. In understanding all the processes that have to shut down, we learn that, unless there is a simple cardiac arrest or sudden death, dying is like being born. It is a miracle in its own right.

As chaplains, you witness people in need of care and ministry from the moment of birth to the moment of death. You represent God, in God's fullest vessel of love. You come from a specific faith tradition, yet you speak to people whose ultimate need transcends both doctrine and creed. As you participate in the mystery of death, your presence will speak much more loudly than creed ever can.

Witnessing death is like witnessing birth. Both represent the ebb and flow of life itself and provide a window into the majesty of creation. May you feel honored to be that witness.

Special Circumstances

1. When a Person Is to Be Taken Off Life Support

Circumstances

More and more, people at the end of their lives are being supported by artificial means. Families and loved ones have to make difficult decisions along the way in accepting feeding tubes, respirators, and other technical means of support while medical treatment continues. Unfortunately, when treatment is no longer effective, it is also up to family members to make the decision that will end the life of their loved one.

Taking someone off life support is an action that can be filled with anguish and guilt for the surviving family. Ironically, it is one of the more peaceful ways a person can die. The body, which has been supported by machines and technology, is suddenly allowed to shut down slowly and naturally. This gives the family time to prepare, both emotionally and spiritually, for the moment of death.

The chaplain or pastoral caregiver can assist the family during this time by working with medical personnel, who generally want the procedure to be as calm and supportive as possible, and by providing a spiritual framework for the entire process.

What You Can Do with the Dying Person

- Explain to the person on life support what is about to happen.
- Talk to the dying person, letting him or her know that it is time to let go.
- Pray on his or her behalf.
- Say good-byes on his or her behalf.
- Offer strength and courage for the journey.
- Perform whatever sacramental rituals (anointing, communion, etc.) are appropriate.

What You Can Do with the Loved Ones

- Create a prayerful atmosphere and a sacred space.
- Allow them to say their good-byes.
- Include them in prayers and sacraments; make this an experience in which the dying person is surrounded by family and friends.
- After good-byes are said, begin the process of vigiling until death occurs.

Be Aware

- Work with the medical staff to understand the parameters of the procedure.
- Try to make this an intimate experience for the family, within the boundaries of the medical unit.
- Understand that once the machines are turned off, death may not happen instantaneously. Families often assume this will happen. Death can take hours or even a few days.
- Be aware that families may not want to be present when the machines are turned off.

- Be sensitive to the fact that families may not want to stay much longer after the machines are turned off.
- Recognize that the person on life support is experiencing a letting go, just like any other person who is dying. Support that process with sacred presence and prayer.

2. When Sudden Death Occurs

Circumstances

Many deaths happen suddenly and without warning. Some happen in emergency rooms and others happen on-site, either in the home or outside a hospital setting. If the person is at the hospital, medical teams go into emergency status and everything is done to save him or her. If death occurs, the chaplain is able to be present and perform any rituals needed. This is a very stressful time and you are often the go-between with the family and loved ones.

What You Can Do Depending on Location

If you are in the emergency room and death is imminent, the activities of medical personnel will take highest priority. You can, however, create a prayerful atmosphere out of the way of the team of workers. Sometimes that is all you can do. If possible, try to access the person's body and lay hands on him or her in prayer. The last rites are always appropriate, even from a distance. Decide whether it is more important to be with the person dying, creating a presence with prayer, or to be with the nearby loved ones. It actually may be more helpful to be in the same room as the person who is dying. Remember, this experience is about the dying person and what he or she is going through. You are the link to the spiritual, and you may have to claim that with assurance and authority.

If death is approaching rapidly and you are outside a medical facility, help the people nearby make any decisions about finding medical help or letting the person die naturally. Your role as chaplain or pastoral caregiver is once again to provide a spiritual space so that the person can die understanding and experiencing the presence of the

Divine. Keep bringing the focus back to prayer and to God.

What You Can Do with the Dying Person

- Pray.
- Lay hands on the person in prayer.
- Find a place in the room to create a sacred space.
- Talk to the person who is dying in a calm and soothing voice.
- When death has occurred and the medical people leave, offer to begin preparation of the body.

What You Can Do with the Loved Ones

- Assure them that you will be present during medical procedures.
- Help them with their own prayers in the midst of their fear and anxiety.
- Help them focus on finding strength and courage for their dying loved one.
- Comfort them.

Be Aware

- You will take last place in the overall dynamics of the medical emergency.
- It is your job to find a place of peace in the midst of the chaos and fear.
- You cannot fix the situation. You can only be present.

Remember, again, that the priority is the person who is dying. In the midst of chaos, that person needs God's presence more than ever.

3. When You Arrive after Death Occurs

Circumstances

Most often, the chaplain or pastoral care worker is called after a death occurs. Either a person has died a short time ago and the family is on its way to be with the body, or the death occurred some distance away and the chaplain has been called to help the family or loved ones pastorally. In either situation, you are not present at the moment of passing.

What You Can Do

Your first inclination is, of course, to respond pastorally to the surviving loved ones, and that is always a chaplain's responsibility. However, there are things that you can do to help the person who has died, even after death has occurred. As discussed previously, preparing the body and sitting with it are always sacred experiences, providing time for family members to come to terms with what has happened and giving the soul an opportunity to make its transition.

When you are with the body:

- Create sacred space around the body and prepare to sit with it for a period of time.
- Offer prayers of commendation for the soul.
- Help the family and loved ones say goodbye.

When you are not able to be with the body:

- Find a symbol that connects the person who has died to the surviving loved ones and use it as a focus for prayer.

- Create a small altar or sacred space and offer prayers or rituals.
- Honor the natural feelings of grief, but bring primary attention to the necessary transition of the soul.
- Help family members understand their experience of the death and how they can assist in letting go.

Be Aware

Many emotions come to the surface when death occurs and you, the spiritual caregiver, are not there. You can help in two parallel ways: in the actual transition of the soul, going from life to death, and in the grieving of the survivors. Our society tends to place its attention on the living. As chaplain, you can honor the process of dying by creating time and space to be with the body. It may be uncomfortable or unfamiliar to us, but spending time with the body has great value for both the survivors and, we trust, for the soul who has died. The community of the living has an honored tradition in helping those who are dying. Space and time are fluid during this mystery, but we can always be present in God's time and process.

✧ APPENDIX B ✧

Recognizing and Understanding the Dying Process

How We Can Support the Dying Person and His or Her Family
—The Reverend Nancy Witt, PT, MSW

Ten years ago, Sherwin Nuland wrote a book entitled *How We Die*. It offered portraits of what the dying process looked like as it occurred in a number of different disease processes, such as heart disease, cancer, and dementia. In its time, the book was revolutionary, because, in the late twentieth century, most Westerners rarely saw death, much less understood the process. Death in our time is something that usually happens in hospital or nursing home rooms, far removed from the nest of the family home where a scant

91

century ago it happened routinely. Few people know the dying process well and thus, when death pays a visit, the dying person and his or her family and friends are often unprepared and consequently fearful.

So, understanding the process of dying becomes central to our own comfort levels with our work in Sacred Dying. If we are knowledgeable about the process, then our level of confidence will buoy up the dying person as well as the family, and help to ease their fears of the unknown.

How, then, shall we understand the dying process? I would like to offer a metaphor that many of us have become more familiar with over the last quarter century. Let us look to the beginning of life, the process of childbirth. A woman in the final days of her pregnancy begins to undergo certain physical, emotional, and yes, even spiritual changes that lead to the birth of her child. Science tells us that the baby is also engaged in a parallel process.

Subtle physiological changes, brought on by the shared chemistry of the mother and the baby, cause the cervix to ripen, soften, and begin to open. These same hormonal and chemical shifts also cause the joints in the mother's pelvis to soften in preparation for the delivery of the child through it, allowing it to spread as necessary. Other hormones prepare the baby's lungs for breathing air. The same hormones that cause the uterus to contract cause the mom's milk to "let down." Neurochemical processes have the baby primed to suck. Other chemicals cause the mom's stools to soften. The mom begins to pace and nest. The baby becomes still and waits.

While we classically think of labor pains or the rupture of the membranes as the hallmarks of the "start" of labor, it is in fact a process, with recognizable "soft signs," that begins well before the first labor pains. By the time labor is easily recognized, it has been underway for some time.

And thus it is with dying.

But for a moment, before considering the dying process, stop and think about life. Think about all the processes that life entails. It is really so miraculous . . . that at the moment of birth, all of the different systems for sustaining life are up and running, even if they are not fine-tuned. The nervous system allows the individual to perceive its world and to interact with it. The respiratory system allows the body to capture and utilize oxygen from the air, and the digestive system turns complex foods into simple chemical elements that, in turn, nurture every cell in the body through the circulatory system. The circulatory system carries nutrients and oxygen everywhere they are needed and then carries away the wastes to other organ systems, which filter and further remove waste and toxins. Then the reproductive system is capable of starting another life. And all of these life processes are wrapped in skin, without which we could not exist. Each of these systems is infused with a life force that is beyond our knowing.

How then shall we die? How is it that all of these complex systems cease to run? What does that look like, and how can we support the person who is going through this process? Let's look at the "soft signs of dying," try to understand each one, and get ideas for our own caregiving. Understand that the timing of death is not entirely predictable, but as more and more of these signs are present, death is more imminent. Once many of these signs are present, death usually follows within approximately four days. But the more signs you recognize, the more important it is to set up and begin the vigiling process.

The Dying Process and How We Can Help

1. *Loss of vital energy.* At the end of life, energy wanes. What does this look like? The dying person may experience increasing periods of sleepiness and, in the end, even coma. He or she will also experience increasing weakness.

How can we help? We can recognize that this decrease of energy is normal and natural. We can support the person in his or her need to sleep, because it allows time to work on unresolved issues through the medium of dreaming. Let the dying person sleep, gathering energy for the remaining wakeful periods. We can share with the loved ones the fact that he or she may sleep and wake much like a newborn, and so it is often helpful to plan to have some-one nearby day and night to meet the dying per-son's physical, emotional, and spiritual needs. If the person has slipped into a coma, it is espe-cially helpful that the family understand that hearing is usually intact; they should assume that their family member hears all that they say. It is good to encourage family members to share their love and support even when the person is comatose.

As the person becomes weaker, caregivers and family members can offer to help with many of the tasks the person was able to do earlier. These tasks may include, but are not limited to: helping with walking or getting around, bathing, toileting, eating and drinking, turning in bed, or gently moving limbs that have become too heavy for the person to lift.

2. *Changes in breathing patterns.* Breathing is a complex neurological process that actually has several redundant backup systems. As the body shuts down, breathing patterns change as the more complex breathing systems stop and the backup systems kick in. There are five different levels of breathing: a) normal breathing; b) Cheyne-Stokes breathing, (a pattern of regular/irregular breathing spells, which can go on for days); c) deep panting as death comes closer; d) agonal breaths, or gasping motions made with the mouth just before death; and finally, e) final cleansing breaths or sighs. Not every person will go through all five. In addition, some people may sound congested depending on how much fluid they are dealing with in their lungs, whether their

lungs are inflamed or they have pneumonia, or if they have aspirated some of their own saliva. This is often called the "death rattle."

How can we help? We can reassure the person who is dying that he or she is okay. We can offer oxygen if it is prescribed and available. We can also reassure the family that these breathing changes are a normal process. It is believed that the dying person may not be aware of his or her breathing, so the family may be more uncomfortable than the person who is dying. If it sounds like the person is struggling with a lot of fluid in his or her lungs, we can look to hospice or to other support persons for guidance regarding how best to help make the person comfortable. Sometimes turning the person from side to side can help breathing; sometimes good oral care may help. Often sponge swabs for wiping out a person's mouth if it is dry will be at the bedside. Lip balm may also help a person to be comfortable. Do not, however, give fluids unless you know it is okay to do so.

3. *Changes in the nervous system.* The dying person's nervous system is also losing vital energy. Sensory organs may not work as well as they once did. Vision may dim. Taste may diminish.

Sensation, especially in the hands and feet, may decrease as circulation shuts down. Neurological changes may occur. Some people seem to hallucinate or see people or things that aren't there, or at least people or things that cannot be seen by everyone else. The last sense that remains, according to research, is hearing.

How can we help? We can provide reassurance to the dying person and to the family that these changes are normal. We can seek to set up the environment so that visitors can sit close by, so that lighting, while not bright, is sufficient for the person to see. We can speak in a normal tone but make sure that we speak clearly. Be sure that the dying person has his or her hearing aid in, if that is appropriate. We can encourage touch if it feels good or doesn't seem to irritate a comatose person: gentle massage, holding someone's hand, soft sheets or blankets; a familiar pillow; soft, familiar music. A soothing bed bath in a warm room, a gentle toweling off, and redressing in clean clothes and changing to fresh sheets can be helpful, as can a soothing rub with lotion if the dying person's skin is dry.

One of the most important things a pastoral caregiver can offer is a reassuring presence through the times when the person seems to be coming and going from the other side. When there is confusion, we can gently reorient the dying person to time and place, but there's no need to force the issue if he or she seems to be somewhere else. If someone is comatose, we can identify ourselves. We can make sure the environment seems safe, that the dying person is not feeling as if he or she is about to fall off a bed or chair or commode.

4. *Changes in circulation and temperature regulation.* As the body shuts down, the center in the brain that regulates temperature may shut down too, or begin to fail. This may mean that the dying person will spike a temperature, and will often mean that he or she looks flushed and sweaty. On the other hand, some people's circulation simply begins to shut down, and their extremities become cool to the touch and pale or mottled in color. This process can begin days or hours before death, and is one of those "soft signs." As circulation shuts down, there may be swelling in certain body parts, or the person may develop pressure sores due to lack of oxygen in skin tissues, especially skin over bony prominences, like heels and elbows.

How can we help? We can reassure the family that these changes are a normal part of the process. If the person is hot and sweaty, we can sponge him or her down with a cool cloth, or lay a fresh cool cloth on the forehead, or behind the neck. We might run a fan. We can ask hospice or medical caregivers if there is medicine that can be given to reduce fever. We can support turning the dying person every couple of hours to prevent bedsores and to improve comfort. However, as death becomes imminent, turning is no longer necessary.

5. *Changes in appetite.* As people approach death, appetite and thirst wane as needs for nutrition diminish. People need less and less to eat or drink. This can be difficult in certain cultures where food until the end is important. The digestive process slows down and may even stop before death. If food or drink is consumed at this point, it may cause painful bloating or other fluid imbalances. As the person weakens, he or she may also have difficulty swallowing, and food or drink may actually cause choking or aspirating of the substance into the lungs.

How can we help? We can reassure the family that a person does not die because he or she has stopped eating; rather, the person stops eating because he or she is dying. If a person is still interested in food, it can be good to offer small amounts of favorite foods. More important may be the reminiscing that goes along with the favorite food. Don't force food or drink. Remember that a dry mouth can be cared for with a moist swab; a wet, cool washcloth; or artificial saliva substitutes. And lip balm may help with dry lips.

6. *Bowel and bladder changes.* As the need for food and fluids diminishes and the digestive system and circulatory systems slow down, the person may become constipated (he or she may also be already constipated if on pain medication) or cease to have bowel movements. Urine production slows down, and the urine may be brown or red in color and very scant as the kidneys also slow down or cease to function. Close to the end, incontinence of the bowel and bladder may be seen.

How can we help? Helping the family to understand that decreased production of urine and diminished bowel movements are also soft signs of dying is a good thing to do. Encouraging scrupulous hygiene following bowel or bladder accidents helps the dying person remain comfortable. Having a bedside commode as long as a person is awake enough to use it can be helpful. In some instances, a catheter is placed in the bladder. If there is tremendous discomfort due to constipation, discuss this with caregivers—they might decide on a procedure such as a suppository or an enema to relieve pressure. If there are Chux pads available, having one beneath the person as death approaches can help should he or she evacuate the bowels at the time of death.

7. *Emotional changes.* The emotional "soft signs" of approaching death are varied and may include an increase in reminiscing. You may also see increased confusion, perhaps because of metabolic changes or perhaps because of increasing episodes of "crossing over" and experiencing the presence of others who have gone before. There is often a clear indication that the dying person's focus is turning inward, that his or her circle of concern is narrowing, and that he or she is losing interest in things beyond immediate needs and concerns. Fear may be expressed verbally, especially if there are unfinished issues or unresolved questions about what is to come. Depression may be seen in folks who aren't ready to go.

Medications can produce agitation or delirium, or these signs can occur naturally, according to the internal process going on. There may be emotional upheaval following dreams as the person works through life review or resolution of long-held inner conflict. Sometimes, personality traits seen throughout a person's lifetime may intensify, or they may even do a complete reversal. For example, a woman who has been quiet and complacent her entire life suddenly insists on choreographing everything happening around her. Many times, we see inhibitions released in the face of death.

How can we help? Recognize that as the power goes out of the body, the mind and spirit may still be active, sorting through and searching for meaning in the dying transition. This is where the process needs what every birth should have: a doula. A doula is a person who sits with the birthing mother. Her presence alone lessens the complication rate immensely. And so it is with death. Our presence is reassuring. Our acceptance and support are vital. We can help family and friends to say the things they need to say, to say good-bye, and especially to express love and forgiveness.

8. *Changes in comfort level: pain.* Obviously, some reasons for death are painful, while others are painless. Controlling pain helps a person to make the transition with dignity and with less fear.

How can we help? We can work with hospice or the caregivers to communicate a person's needs vis-à-vis pain. There is no need for anyone to suffer.

9. *Changes in language.* As we approach death, we bring our unique history and language experiences with us. As each of us begins that experience, we will undergo our own transition, experiencing our dying as only we can. How each person expresses what is going on internally is completely unique to that person.

How can we help? Listen. Listen for the words that speak of the transition. Listen for the metaphors for death that the dying have learned in their lives. Are they headed for the "pearly gates"? Do they want to "go home"? Pay attention as people attempt to describe the indescribable experience they are having. It is as close to heaven as we will ever get on earth. Watch your own language and the language of family members. Are we holding them here, or are we releasing them to move on into the light? This is a precious time when, it is said, the veil between life and death is thin. Be alert. Be present. Support and encourage.

✧ RESOURCES ✧

Anderson, Megory. *Sacred Dying: Creating Rituals for Embracing the End of Life*. New York: Marlowe & Co., 2003.

Billings, Alan. *Dying and Grieving: A Guide to Pastoral Ministry*. London: SPCK, 2002.

Byock, Ira. *Dying Well: The Prospect for Growth at the End of Life*. New York: Riverhead Books, 1998.

Callanan, Maggie, and Patricia Kelley. *Final Gifts: Understanding the Special Awareness, Needs, and Communications of the Dying*. New York: Bantam Books, 1997.

Cohen, Cynthia, et al. *Faithful Living, Faithful Dying: Anglican Reflections on End of Life*

Care. Harrisburg, PA: Morehouse Publishing, 2000.

Holder, Jennifer Sutton, and Jann Aldredge-Clanton. *Parting: A Handbook for Spiritual Care Near the End of Life*. Chapel Hill: University of North Carolina Press, 2004.

Johnson, Christopher Jay, and Marsha G. McGee. *How Different Religions View Death and Afterlife. 2nd ed.* Philadelphia: Charles Press, 1998.

Kalina, Kathy. *Midwife for Souls: Spiritual Care for the Dying*. Boston: Pauline Books & Media, 1993.

Nuland, Sherwin B. *How We Die: Reflections on Life's Final Choices*. New York: Vintage, 1995.

Smith, Harold Ivan. *Finding Your Way to Say Good-bye: Comfort for the Dying and Those Who Care for Them*. Notre Dame, IN: Ave Maria Press, 2002.

Smith, Rodney. *Lessons from the Dying*. Boston: Wisdom Publications, 1998.

Stanworth, Rachel. *Recognizing Spiritual Needs in People Who Are Dying.* Oxford: Oxford University Press, 2004.

Stillwater, Michael, and Gary Malkin, producers. *Graceful Passages: A Companion for Compassionate Transition.* Wisdom of the World Productions.

Zonnebelt-Smeenge, Susan, and Robert C. De Vries. *Living Fully in the Shadow of Death.* Grand Rapids, MI: Baker Books, 2004.